Flitter, Flutter Butterfly

Written By Sandra Rye Baggett

Illustrated By Nancy Vinson Nave

To order additional copies of this book, contact:
Xlibris
1-888-795-4274
www.Xlibris.com
Orders@Xlibris.com

Dedication:

For Drew............................and Seth

This book is dedicated to my children, Lee and Ryen Baggett, and my grandchildren, Drew and Seth Baggett. Thank you for letting me read and sing to you when you were all young. This book was inspired by Drew. When she was 5 years old, she asked me to make up a song about a butterfly. This is what I came up with. We sang this song almost every Friday. I also sang it to Seth when he was small. I used it in my kindergarten classroom as well. My hope is that your child will enjoy this song and the pictures. I love you Drew and Seth, and hope your children will someday enjoy this book as well.
Love, Mamaw
Sandra Rye Baggett

For Mac............................and Lucas

To my children, Lucibeth and Beau, and my grandchildren, Mac and Lucas: Thank you for encouraging me; for being the butterflies in my life!
Love you, Nana
Nancy Vinson Nave

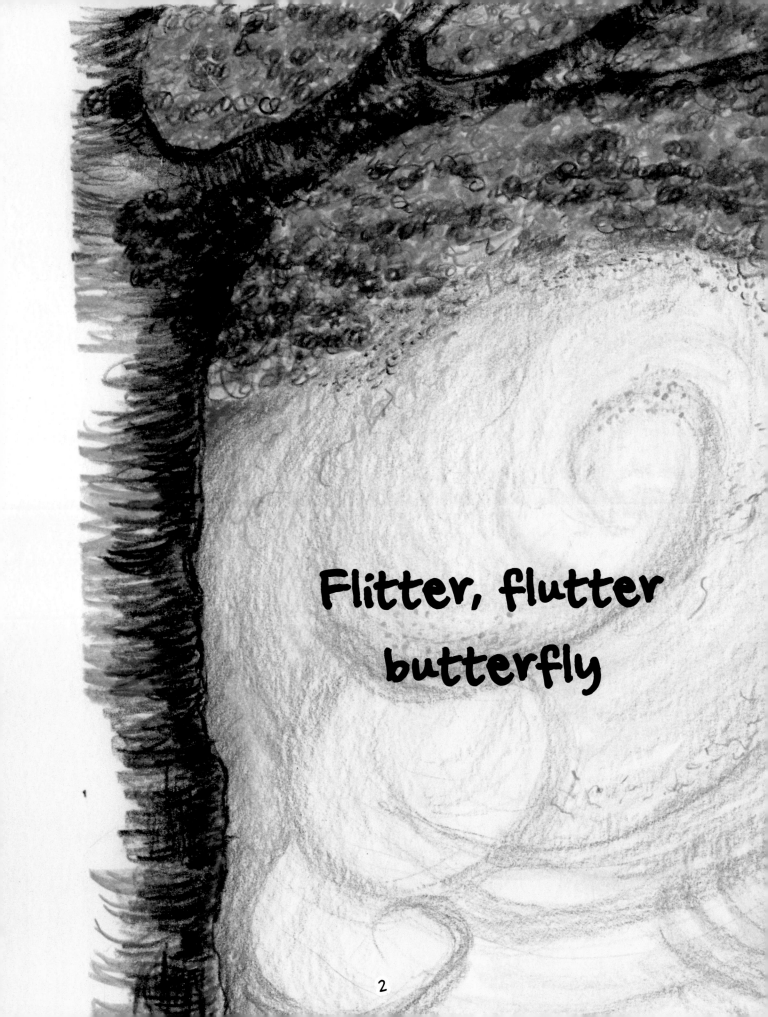

Flitter, flutter
butterfly

Flying through
the air.

Flitter, flutter
butterfly

Won't you land
somewhere?

Lift your wings up
to the sky,
Flitter, flutter
butterfly.

Flitter, flutter butterfly!

Flitter, Flutter Butterfly

Instructions for Music and Dance:

- Ask someone to play this song for you, or you may make up your own tune.
- Can you move around like a butterfly?
- Make up a dance to go with your song.
- "Flitter, flutter" like a butterfly!

Parent Help Pages

- As you read this book to your child, ask questions:

  1. Can you find the butterflies in this book?

  2. Where is the chrysalis?

  3. Can you find the caterpillar?

  4. Where are the eggs the mother butterfly laid on a leaf?

  5. What hatches from the eggs? (caterpillar)

  6. When the caterpillar makes the chrysalis, what will happen inside? (The caterpillar will metamorphose into a butterfly.)

  7. Why does a mother butterfly lay her eggs on the leaf? (The caterpillar will have food to eat when it hatches.)

- A butterfly is an insect. How can you tell an insect from other animals? (It has 3 body parts: head, thorax, and abdomen; 2 antenna which are usually straight; 6 legs; often wings; and lays eggs to reproduce. It also goes through metamorphosis.)

- How are butterflies helpful? (Butterflies are helpful because they carry pollen from the flowers of plants and pollinate other plants.)

- How are butterflies and moths different? (Most butterflies fly during the day and rest at night (diurnal). Moths fly at night and rest during the day (nocturnal). Moths have larger bodies than butterflies, and their antennae are thick and feathery. Butterflies have thin, straight antennae.)

- Allow your child to draw a butterfly. Remember the body has 3 parts: head, abdomen, and thorax. Wings are alike and the same size. Finish with crayons, paint, or other media.

Fun Art with Butterflies

A. Make a caterpillar from an egg carton. Cut and paint to decorate. Cut pipe cleaners for legs. Use moveable eyes if you desire.

B. Trace your child's hands and put them together to make a butterfly. Color the body and decorate the wings.

C. Trace your child's feet and cut them out of paper. Put them together to make a butterfly. Make the toes point up. The body of the butterfly can be cut and glued into place or colored/painted. Antenna can be added with pipe cleaners or drawn.

Compare and Contrast
Butterflies and Moths

A. **Butterflies** are active during the day (diurnal).

B. **Moths** are active at night (nocturnal).

A. **Caterpillars** spin chrysalides.

B. **Moths** form cocoons using thread from their bodies and dry leaves.

A. **Caterpillars** take about 7-10 days before they make their chrysalides.

B. **Moths** take several weeks before they make their cocoons.

A. **Caterpillars** stay in the chrysalis stage for 7-10 days.

B. **Moths** stay in the cocoon from a few weeks to a few months, depending on the temperature of the weather.

A. **Butterflies** have 2 straight antennae.

B. **Moths** have feathery antennae.

A. **Butterflies** are insects.

B. **Moths** are insects.

A. **Butterflies** have 3 body parts, 6 legs, 2 antennae, and 2 wings.

B. **Moths** have 3 body parts, 6 legs, 2 antennae, and 2 wings.

A. **Adult butterflies** eat nectar from flowers.

B. **Adult Luna Moths** do not eat.

Building a Butterfly/Moth House

Supplies Needed:

- Old aquarium or large cardboard box
- Twig or small branch
- Small plastic Dixie cup
- Paper towels or sponge
- Netting or cheesecloth for cover
- Caterpillars (see Acknowledgement Page to order)
- Sugar

1. If using an aquarium, skip to step 3.

2. If using a cardboard box, cut one side off the box. On the back side of the box, cut a flap large enough to reach inside to feed the butterflies. Using a pencil punch a row of air holes on each side of the box. Decorate the box.

3. Place a large twig on the bottom of the butterfly/moth house at a 45 degree angle. (lean against the side of the box or aquarium.)

4. If you order caterpillars from Carolina Biological Supply Co., follow directions as given. Wait until all caterpillars have spun their chrysalides before moving them to the house. It is important to not disturb the chrysalis during formation. Securely tape netting over the top of the box or aquarium.

5. Butterflies will emerge in 7 to 10 days. Release them back to the environment within a week. Put food in the house when they hatch, Mix 2 teaspoons of sugar in 1 cup of water. Place the solution in the Dixie cup. Roll a paper towel to

make a wick and place in the solution. Be sure the wick is higher than the cup. A sponge would also work.

6. If you order a Luna Moth from Carolina Biological Supply Co., it will come in the cocoon stage. It takes 2 or 3 weeks for a moth to hatch. Follow the instructions as given. The life span of the Luna Moth is only 1 week and does not have to be fed. After watching for a day or so, release it back into the environment. Release it in the evening or night, as they are nocturnal insects. Do not put the moths and butterflies in the same house together.

7. Make your child a butterfly/moth journal by using a notebook or loose leaf paper. Write the date on each page. Have your child look for butterflies and moths. When they see one, ask them to draw what they see in the journal. Add a description of the weather. Create a story or poem to go with the picture.

Butterfly Anatomy

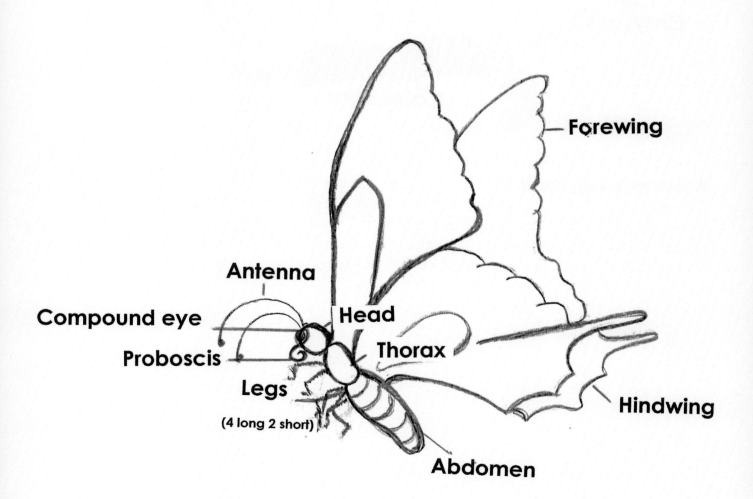

Life Cycle of the Butterfly

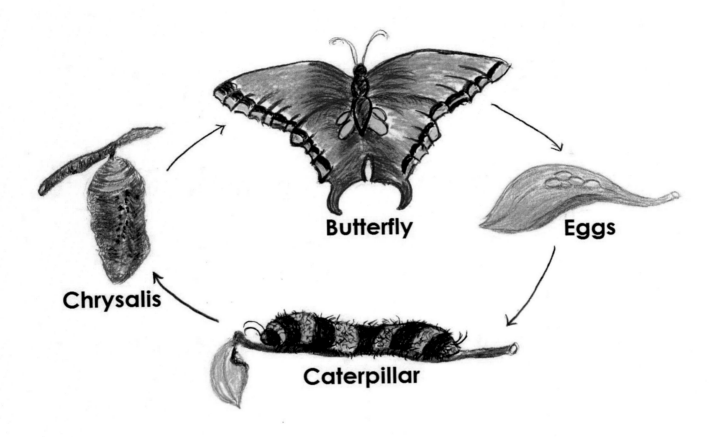

Butterfly

Eggs

Chrysalis

Caterpillar

What is metamorphosis? (The life cycle of a butterfly begins with the mother laying her eggs on a leaf. The caterpillars hatch from the eggs. They eat and grow. As they grow, they shed their skins.   Eventually they spin a chrysalis with thread from their bodies and hide inside while their bodies go through a change from caterpillar into a butterfly. This process is called metamorphosis.)

Acknowledgements

The How to Build a Butterfly/Moth House project in this book came from the Earth's Birthday Project, P.O. Box 1536, Santa Fe, NM 87504.
Phone no: 1-800-698-4438   Website: http://www.earthbirthday.org

To order caterpillars or cocoons contact: Carolina Biological Supply Co., 2700 York Rd., Burlington, NC 27215
Phone no: 1-800-334-5551   Website: www.carolina.com

Photography courtesy of James Gray: james@jamesgraystudios.com for photo on the back cover.

Interesting websites where your child can see the life cycle of a Luna Moth can be found on Youtube.

If you are interested in ordering a CD with the music, please contact Sandra Baggett at: lcsbaggett@gmail.com

Printed in the United States
By Bookmasters